Secrets

of

River

Fishing

By
Jerry E. Sneath

$\mathcal{CP}$ Catlett
Publishing

Secrets of River Fishing
©1995 by Jerry E. Sneath

Catlett Publishing
P.O. Box 32
Bellwood, PA 16617

*Library of Congress
Catalog Card No.
95-71834*

DEDICATION

I dedicate this book to all rivermen and in particular Bill Schirf, George Rexford, and my son Lance, who have tolerated me all these years. Bill has given of his time to proofread this book for me. I also recognize the contributions my father, Robert E. Sneath, has made during the years of my youth teaching me a love for the outdoors.

I would like to remember my Mother, Anna E. Sneath, who spent long hard hours pointing my life in the right direction.

It is with deep appreciation that I give thanks to my daughter Tammy, who has designed and arranged this book and my son Vince, who has come through for me with the proper maps to find the area of specific rivers I wanted to investigate. Finally, I want to thank my wife Sue, who puts up with my fishing and hunting, fosters my hopes and dreams, and gives of her time to act as my personal secretary.

TABLE OF CONTENTS

In this era of doing even recreation at a quick pace, it took me a number of years to fully develop into a better than average river fisherman. In an age where so many people think they are experts in one thing or another, I have slowly realized the successful methods of river fishing I have learned over the last 40 years have really evolved as a result of a lot of trial and error.

The philosophy of fishing discussed in this book will work in every river each season. The techniques mentioned in this book have enabled me to catch an average of 75 smallmouth bass on numerous occasions when I travel to a local river.

This book is going to deal with rivers of small, medium, and large size. In reality what is explained here will be found useful no matter what species of fish you are trying to catch. It is my assumption you as a fisherman are reading this book because you fish, or would like to spend some time fishing rivers, or that you live near a river. I am going to present to you the methods I have found to be so successful in the rivers of Pennsylvania, West Virginia, North Carolina, and Texas.

CHAPTER 1

Basic River Fishing

The first thing a fisherman must realize is fish are extremely sensitive to what goes on around them. A successful river fisherman is patient, quiet, and somewhat secretive. He knows that a river is basically shallow and that sounds in the water are picked up by the fish. Any sound that is not natural will place the fish on alert and will probably send them to the bottom hiding beside or under rocks, logs, and any other protection they can find.

One of the worst times to attempt river fishing is around a major national holiday as many fishermen are on the river with their boats pounding the bottom. Avoiding weekends, if possible, is also good but if this is the only time you have, then pay particular attention to the things I emphasize throughout this book.

I indicated to you that not making noise is really important. It is also important to take your time in fishing. Patience is extremely important. The first thing I want you to know is what I call the 100 yard rule. This is where you spend your time fishing approximately 100 yards of river. The key here is not any section of river but a part of the river that should hold fish. In our country most rivers that are not completely disrupted by dams have three areas to be considered. They are riffles, holes, and runs. I will go into detail how each section of the river plays a role in supporting the fish population throughout the year. In each part of the country, there are certain species of fish found in the river. The local fishermen who are successful understand the species of fish they are after as well as how they fit into the sections of the river during the year.

Since I spend most of my fishing time in Pennsylvania fishing for smallmouth bass, I will use certain techniques for smallmouth that can be used in rivers elsewhere for channel catfish, white bass, brown trout, and many other species.

I am a bait fisherman. Bait fishing has had bad publicity lately, particularly among certain groups of anglers. It is not my desire or goal to attack other anglers or their methods. In fact, in order to protect our sport, I believe outdoor sportsmen must unite. I will explain what bait I use as the book develops. If you follow me back to sections of the river I mentioned, remember a river will have riffles, holes, and runs. Rivers with a steeper fall will have shorter distance between the sections. Slow moving rivers will have long slow runs, and in them it is more difficult to locate concentrations of fish.

The first thing I do in fishing a new river is drive along it and, if possible, stop every mile or so and look at that section. If I find a section which interests me, I mark a highway map or draw a map to place a particular area for future study. I may even go further. If the river has a lot of remote sections far from the highway, I take a float trip with my maps and notebook. Notice I do not fish on the float trip. One of the ways of attempting to fish a river is the over-publicized float trip. I never worry about floaters catching large numbers of fish. River fishing is a slow process and floating is way too fast.

My next move then is to examine a stretch of river I feel is a potential fish producer. I prefer areas that require some physical effort to reach. One thing to keep in mind is a stretch of river that has a highway alongside it is fished much more heavily than an area that takes some walking. If at all possible, my first time into the new area is during a low water period. Then I can see most of the rocks and other obstructions that provide cover for fish and in my case smallmouth bass.

If the river is small or medium size, you may fish it primarily by wading. I have found a fisherman can be much more secretive by wading. I try to avoid wading if it creates waves in the water. This will put down the fish quickly. Fish have a lateral line along their sides and pick up all kinds of vibrations in the water. When I wade into a hole or run, I will usually go extremely slow as if I am stalking a game animal. I have found that standing still for a long period in the same pool has been extremely important in my success.

In the average day of fishing, I will very seldom travel a distance of 100 yards. It is not a rare day I will catch and release as many as 75 bass, sometimes catching several bass on one minnow. I will go into detail later, but let me tell you now that I use what most fisherman would call minnows as my bait. I used to use crayfish and hellgramites and still believe they are good bait, but my experience with minnows has proven they will produce catches of larger fish more consistently.

The term minnow is so inclusive that much study by a river fisherman is necessary to understand that just any minnow will not do. Most of the minnows sold in bait stores work very poorly. Many can hardly be kept alive until you get them to the river, and some others are so unnatural that only small fish will be caught on them.

Getting back to my first trip into the section of river being considered as serious fishing water, I have found that exploring by wading and fishing enables me to study the river. The depth, type of bottom, and potential for food sources of various species of game fish can be explored. I may cross and experience the opposite side of the river. Many times, because of current flow and the rock structure fishing, one side of the pool is much more productive than the other. This may be discovered the first time out or after several trips into the area.

I believe it is necessary to fish a certain section of river several times before I decide to write it off as a serious producer. Remember that this section of river has the type of structure and food the smallmouth needs. I fish it several times because sometimes the fish are simply not biting. If river conditions are right and I will describe what I mean by "right," I rarely have a day when less than 25 bass are caught.

If the river is large or deep, I don't wade but use a jon boat with either poles or oars. Avoid noise, waves, and splashing, as much as humanly possible. If the water is clear, forget the boat and stay on shore. Nothing angers me more than to have other fishermen bang around and float over the area I am fishing as if they are not disrupting the fish. Fish, waiting for something to eat, are not as stupid as many anglers assume them to be.

This is an example of a tributary of a river where minnows can be caught that are naturally found in the watershed. In this case this is actually the upper part of the Juniata River and many good fish bait have been taken from this region.

This picture shows a mature river with a riffle that indicates not much of a gradient drop. The hole below this type of riffle is quite shallow and not very productive.

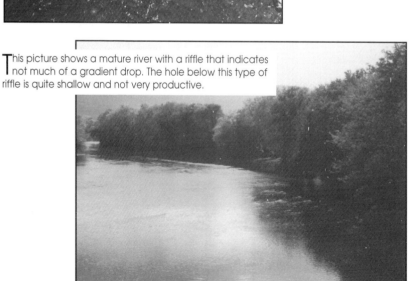

The typical river structure of riffle, pool, and run is very obvious in this photo. This is a young river that has a relatively steep gradient and cooler water. Both brown trout and smallmouth bass are found here. This is a transition area and throughout the year there are times when both species of fish may be stressed because of water temperatures. Spawning may occur very irregularly for either species.

A more mature river will have a less steep gradient and usually will have long runs before the next set of riffles. In many cases these long runs contain no or only small fish. A river fisherman may look carefully at the section just before the next riffle. In addition large rocks or logs may produce a pocket that holds fish. If the angler takes time to investigate these runs it may prove to be worth their effort.

CHAPTER 2

Equipment and Techniques

The selection of the right equipment for river fishing is determined by the size of the adversary, the preference of the fisherman, and possibly the river itself.

I have found both medium and light action spinning rods have met my needs for the type of fishing I do. Even when I use the light action rods, I use larger open-faced spinning reels than are normally used with them. I find the smaller sized reels do not hold enough line to fish rivers, they are better suited to trout streams.

I have a personal liking for the shorter rods, 5 to 6 foot ones, rather than longer ones, although both my fishing buddies George and Bill prefer longer rods. Ultralight tackle is too light, and the rod does not have the stiffness essential to set the hook on a fish that is 50 to 75 yards out in the river. My oldest son Lance tried ultralight while on one trip and had to borrow my extra rod and reel to finish the day. I have also found the composite rods of graphite and fiberglass do extremely well.

One thought I want you to keep in mind is river fishing is hard both on the fisherman and his tackle. I have yet to find a reel that will last more than one season of heavy fishing. It is very important to carry an extra reel at least in your vehicle to avoid a ruined fishing trip. I always carry in my truck a complete extra rod and reel. Rivers are extremely hard on tackle because of the fact that as you wade, you may get your reel in the water, and it seems that small grains of sand get into the gears. Buy as good equipment as you can afford without spending the kids lunch money or the money for the electric bill.

Your fishing line also should be of high quality and of sufficient strength to land large fish. Many companies produce fine line. I think the copolymer line is extremely good. I like line that is clear and of small diameter. I have been using 10 lb. test line for the last 15 years. I still have fish that overwhelm the drag and will snap the line from time to time. This usually happens three or four times a season.

Silver Thread line has been my choice for several years now because I find it seems to be very good for the price. If you buy line on bulk spools, you can save a considerable amount of money particularly if you change line as often as I do. I feel the line gets a lot of frayed areas from the rocks in the river. Nothing is more devastating than losing a nice fish as a result of a worn line. I change line after about two weeks of fishing.

I use loose hooks and tie them directly to the line using the modified cinch knot. Most of my hooks are in three sizes—6, 4, and 2. One can buy several hundred and have enough for all season. I made the transition from cheap hooks to the better brand after having some large bass snap the hooks instead of breaking the line. I have found the Mustad or Eagle Claw hooks are quite good. I prefer bait holder hooks with the eye turned in. After using straight eyed and those with the eye turned out, it is my feeling that I get better hooking with a turned in eye.

The only other requirement is to have split-shot provide

enough weight to get the bait down to the fish. The size and number are determined by the river conditions. One thing to keep in mind is you try to present the bait as naturally as possible. It is important to realize a river fisherman is going to lose a lot of terminal tackle because of the rocks and the current. In many cases the fisherman will have to change the number and size of split-shot in order to get the minnow to bounce along the bottom of the river. The main thought to place in your mind is the minnow should be alive but appear injured. Many species of game fish including the smallmouth bass want live food.

The way in which you present the bait will either make it appear natural or the minnow will look unusual, and the larger fish will avoid it as if it's the plague. Many fisherman have to learn that river fishing involves a technique of fishing cross current instead of casting upstream as many trout fisherman do. In river fishing casting upstream will cause a lot of hangups on the bottom and the loss of terminal tackle or the minnow. As the minnow or other bait reaches the end of its sweep downstream, gradually lift the tip of the rod and reel in a couple feet of line. This should be a slow process in order to encourage fish following the bait to strike at that time.

I usually do this same technique except for reeling during the sweep of the bait downstream while holding the line with the index finger of the hand holding the rod. Fish may pick up the bait, and depending on the water temperature, they may swim rapidly away (fishermen call this making a run), or if the water is extremely cold, the fish may simply stay in place and swallow the bait. Experience with each species of fish and the knowledge of the temperature range for activity will help you determine how to react. In early summer and late fall, I attempt to hook the smallmouth as it stops the line. Many fishermen do not even realize they have had a strike.

Another technique that has to be considered is the use of large minnows. In this case a method that works extremely well is to allow the fish to make two runs with the bait. The reason this is necessary is the fish will move away from other fish on the first run and then stop. In the case of smallmouth bass, they will spit out the minnow and take it head first and start their second run. The fisherman should be alert to set the hook when the fish makes the second run and tightens the line. It is important to really set the hook in this situation as there is a lot of slack line between the rod tip and the fish. Earlier I mentioned ultra lite tackle is not a good selection for river fishing and the above-mentioned situation is the major reason. My fishing buddy Bill uses swivels to keep his line from twisting. He also feels the swivel helps to present the minnow more realistically. This is something that you can experiment with and decide for yourself. I tend to avoid a lot of the hassle of tying on extra equipment. In the use of the swivel, the fisherman does avoid a lot of line twist which possibly can weaken the line and destroy its flexibility. I hold the minnow out of the water and let it spin the twist out of the line every two or three cast which seems to work very well for me.

In looking at the natural bait, let me discuss what I feel is extremely important. My fishing friends and I limit our bait to what is found in the watershed we are fishing. This is not unusual, but with the amount of energy needed to get that natural bait, many bait fisherman will go to a bait shop and buy what they have available. In fishing the rivers of Pennsylvania, I go to the tributaries of the particular river I am fishing and catch my minnows. In this case one of the bait fish selected are small minnows of three or four inches in length. They are hardy and will swim and stay alive for a long time.

I usually go the day before and catch my bait. In my garage Bill and I have a pair of laundry tubs with a commercial aerator. This is the same as the bait stores have to keep their minnows alive. In Pennsylvania a fisherman is only permitted to have 50 fish bait and bait fish combined. It is necessary at all times to keep separate containers to avoid fines from the fish commission. Check your own state regulations before you get involved in placing large numbers of minnows in one container.

The next step is to get fish to the river alive. The best method we have found is to place the bait fish in the modern styrofoam minnow bucket or small styrofoam coolers that have snap on lids and drop in several ice cubes. We have also found taping the lids down on the minnow buckets with duct tape helps avoid spilling water in the vehicle.

At the fishing site, we have found that a floating minnow bucket is extremely good to keep the bait alive for fishing. This bucket can be attached to the belt of a wading fisherman or kept attached over the side of a jon boat.

Getting the minnow on the hook while standing in the river can sometimes be frustrating. My buddies and I usually hold a fine meshed landing net under the bait as we hook it through the lips. We also feel that a fine meshed net does not injure the fish as much as larger mesh ones, and this is quite important for any fish you are returning to the river.

When hooking the minnow, two things must be considered. The first is the size of hook to use. We usually use a size 6 or 4 for minnow in the three or four inch range and a size 2 for larger chubs or suckers. The second thing is to make sure that the bait fish is hooked through both lips, or it will get off or be thrown off when you cast.

There definitely is a correlation between the size of the bait used and the fish caught although a medium size smallmouth, twelve to fifteen inches, will take a five inch chub or sucker. It is necessary to warn you about certain smells on your hands. Never spray sun screen or insect repellent and touch the line, hooks, or bait. This will simply turn the fish off and in some cases will also kill your minnows.

Many river fisherman in my area who use natural bait concentrate on crayfish because almost all bass when gutted will have crayfish in them. Softshell crayfish are definitely good fish bait, but the effort to get them is extremely high. We have found the bass will hit minnows more often during the daylight hours, because it is more difficult for the fish to catch minnows. They feed on crawfish, hellgramites, and other freshwater nymphs because they can catch them more easily. During the daylight hours I have discovered that the larger bass will pass up the fishbait and grab the larger minnows if presented properly.

In the river system we primarily fish a 10 lb. channel cat or a 4 lb. smallmouth is a good catch. All of the really large fish I have caught have been on large minnows. I am talking about consistent catches. It is unusual for me to catch less than one hundred bass in a season between twelve and twenty inches. Keep in mind this is fishing public access water which is heavily fished. I avoid advertising a place where I fish and only fish with two or three friends who have the same philosophy as I. We will return to the river very carefully most of the bass we catch although my wife and I do enjoy some good bass filets. In a later chapter, I will discuss catch and release as well as keeping fish.

My fishing buddies and I do not fish the same section of

river constantly as this can be very harmful, not because of us, but because it attracts attention from other fishermen. If they are floating through and constantly see the same fishermen in a particular hole or run, they will connect that we are doing quite well in that area. I never tell other fishermen passing me how well I am doing because that will draw a crowd to that area of the river. Let me emphasize I do this to protect that area of the river. If fishing from the river bank into a particular pool, avoid leaving evidence of being there such as fork sticks that you propped your rods on. If at all possible, tie your boat to a tree and fish from it to avoid developing paths into a favorite fishing spot you have located.

Many times during the winter months, we will explore a section of river looking for new fishing areas. It is good to take pictures of particular pools so that current can be studied and obstructions can be located. Keep in mind these obstructions to river flow provide good resting habitat for the fish, and also the bait fish they consume. This is only preliminary information as each river section must be examined, and as indicated early in this chapter, the 100 yard rules will apply in most cases. Rarely has a day of fishing involved covering more than that distance.

CHAPTER 3

River
Conditions

Water level and clarity are two of the most important conditions to consider in being a successful river fisherman. If the water is extremely high and muddy, my friends and I don't even bother attempting to fish. If the river is normally slightly off-color, that is an extremely different story. If a river has gone from normal summer levels for mid July or August to being somewhat high and off color, we will then fish the riffles instead of the pools. Some of the largest bass can be caught at this time as they feel safe moving into the riffles during the daylight hours to feed on minnows and small gamefish.

Cannibalism is not unusual in most species. Many times channel catfish, bass, and brown trout will move into the riffles at night to feed, but when the water is off color, daytime feeding in these area is frequent. The reason many fish have crawfish as part of their stomach contents is because of this shallow water feeding. Crayfish are actively searching for food at night and are out from under the rocks.

The early part of the season for many species is not as productive for several reasons. If the river and the species of fish being pursued is well known, fishermen will not lose patience or interest in a section of river because of lack of success during the early part of the season. This is particularly true of some of the species of fish that feed more aggressively as the water temperature rises to 70 degrees Fahrenheit or more and the water level drops.

Each species of fish has optimum temperatures for increasing their metabolic rates. The water temperature is also very important for triggering spawning. Each species of fish has water temperature limits for spawning and for feeding. Make the effort to find these ranges for the fish that you are pursuing.

River fishermen also should watch carefully for spawning beds; many species will spawn in the shallow edges of the river. In some cases you can get an idea of the number and size of the fish such as bass by the beds. Try to avoid wading or damaging the beds during the actual spawning season.

I would like to continue with the discussion of the water conditions as the fishing season progresses throughout the summer. It is not unusual during late season for river levels to be extremely low. This can be a very successful but challenging time to fish. The fisherman must be much more cautious in his approach and display a lot more patience. One should avoid moving in the water as much as possible as wave action is really emphasized during low water. All sounds should be kept to a minimum.

In many cases the fish are concentrated in the deeper pools, and fishing without weight is a very good procedure at this time. This permits the minnow to swim freely and is more attractive to the fish. If there is any time when I use lighter weight line, it is at this time. I have occasionally gone to six lb. test during extremely low river levels. Many times under these conditions I have only caught one decent size fish and then they would shut off (quit biting). It is not unusual that after catching a good fish, only small fish will take your bait. Many fishermen never notice this or think they are just not catching the big one. The biggest fish did not get the size they are by being stupid.

If a lot of splashing occurs as a result of fighting a nice fish for several minutes I may move to a different area of the pool or run rather than scare the fish. If I feel the fish are extremely concentrated in the deepest part of the hole, I will take a break rather than catch a number of small ones and create more noise. Many fishermen seem to think they can go into a river and catch the larger fish with ease.

I have several acquaintances that tell me that George, Bill, and I are really lucky. I guess they would rather think this than the fish outsmarted them. Sitting and watching the river and the wildlife around is sometimes more productive than continual fishing and stirring the river. If the river has a layer of silt on the rocks, and you wade through it and stir it up, this simply warns the fish and they sometimes avoid feeding for hours.

This past summer another fishing buddy and I fished a small river that was low and clear. The smallmouth bass were quite visible in the deeper poles, some as deep as seven or eight feet. I simply refused to fish as I knew the bass were down on the bottom just finning and not feeding. My friend tried and tried from one hole to the next to get a response. I learned about the river, and saw some impressive fish without getting myself frustrated because I could not catch them. The next time I visit that section will be when the water is higher and cloudy. This particular river has a mixture of wild brown trout and smallmouth bass. This shows the normal temperature range of the water is such that it will support both species, but it is probably water where one species or the other has some difficult periods during the year maybe even at spawning time.

Many fishermen will change the type of bait they use when the water level is at different stages. I have found I can consistently be just as successful continuing to use minnows, but the way I present them may be altered. The minnows may be fished on the bottom by adding additional split shot or different areas of the run, the lower section of the area fished before the next riffle may hold the fish during high water. The serious angler should spend as much time as possible studying the river bottom in the areas fished in order to know where to fish as water levels change.

I am convinced learning to read a river comes from experience. My son Lance was in the Army stationed at Fort Bragg, North Carolina. We spent some time fishing several of the rivers in that state. Even though it was a strange area to me, we were able to do quite well fishing several of the rivers including the Cape Fear, the Deep, and the Roanoke. Each of these gave us nice catches of largemouth bass and channel catfish. Lance would scout out areas of the river and describe them to me, and we would decide how to fish them when I visited. We would apply the riffle, hole, and run rule with each. In some cases, because the gradient of fall is so gradual, the runs would be extremely long. These runs are usually very unproductive for fishing.

One of the fantastic rivers in North Carolina is the French Broad River in the mountains near Asheville. This is a real sleeper with very little fishing pressure. It is a river that contains smallmouth bass and channel cats. I would not be surprised if a record smallmouth would be caught there in the near future. The French Broad River has a steep gradient and has short distances between each hole. The problem with this type of river is any rain in the mountains will cause a very rapid rise in the water level. This type of river system should be avoided till late summer.

Many species of fish including channel and the blue catfish will move about in rivers primarily on a seasonal basis and catching them consistently requires an understanding of their movements. From spring through early summer, they will be spread out, and as fall approaches, they will move back to the deepest holes in the river usually below riffles with steep dropoffs. Some channel cats may move several miles in a season.

The opposite is true of the bass family. The smallmouth will spend its entire life in a one hundred yard long stretch of river. River fishermen should know as much as possible about the species of fish they are attempting to catch. With the knowledge of smallmouth bass, my fishing buddies and I will only remove certain sizes and numbers of fish from a pool during each season. It is extremely irresponsible in a small river to consistently fish the same pools week after week and keep large numbers of fish. Certain species of fish that depend primarily on natural reproduction are easily depleted. I feel that as you develop into a better river fisherman, you respect the fishery and have a better idea of the numbers of fish in a certain area of the river.

I fish a certain area on a medium sized river where I catch as many as 150 bass in 4-6 hours of fishing. The fish are mostly in the 9-12 inch range with an occasional 14 inch fish. Removing some of the 12 inch fish here only helps by providing a better environment for the remaining fish. In another section of the same river, catching 20-30 bass is more the rule. Fishing pressure is the reason. However, the area just mentioned is where I catch 18-20 inch small-mouth bass, usually several each season. This indicates two things. The first is even though fewer fish are in this section, there are some that get large by being difficult to catch, and secondly, they get larger because they have less competition for food.

This riffle forming a pool is much steeper and a good fishing hole is just below the riffle. If it is in an easily accessible region of the river it is probably heavily fished.

This scene shows fishermen is a boat fishing a good area at the end of a run. Many fishermen find that there is a deeper area with large rocks where good size fish such as smallmouth bass and channel cats congregate. This is because the river current speeds up here and more food is brought into the area.

CHAPTER 4

Fishing
With Others

I have few friends when it involves fishing because most of the anglers I know do not fish as I do. This is not saying that their methods are wrong; they are just not my methods. My fishing buddies and I do not go out at the crack of dawn fishing very often. In fact, much of my very successful river fishing occurs between 9 am and 4 pm.

We do fish after dark if we are fishing a particular river or area of a river for catfish. It is important one's fishing friends are aware a time clock is not controlling how much time is spent on the river. I usually give my wife an approximate time to expect me home, but not down to the definite minute.

If you have acquaintances who ask you about fishing or want to fish with you, spend some time talking about the type of fishing they do rather than your own techniques. If you fish with a person that works with you or who is a neighbor, do not start out by taking him to your favorite fishing spots. If it turns out you prefer fishing without that person because of differences in philosophy, you don't want to be finding that person in your spot every time you go there.

An even worse scenario is to find that all of your special fishing pools have been fished out because the person you showed them to is extremely greedy. The friends I fish with all respect the river and realize an area can be hurt severely if it is overfished.

The fishing companions one fishes with must have similar fishing techniques or the pleasure of angling together is lost. Philosophical differences in how to fish and how many fish to keep can lead to a very unhappy time.

My fishing buddies and I are all very conscious of the environment. A "litter bug" would not be welcomed on a trip with any of us. None of my friends and I would ignore an acquaintance trashing the outdoors. It is difficult to understand how some people can be so neat at home and be so particular about their back yard and yet discard trash along a stream as if that is acceptable behavior. An angler who loves the outdoors will be unhappy with this type of companion and will probably get into a conflict. The only other alternative is to follow the person picking up after them.

I try to avoid greedy people and prefer not to hunt and fish with that type of person because not only is greediness a disturbing characteristic, it can also be dangerous. Many times an angler who is more concerned with filling his creel than enjoying the river will do risky things that could lead to injury or death.

An angler trying to teach younger people the pleasure of fishing should be especially careful of their fishing companions. So many fishermen forget that tomorrow is another day and that the experiences we have today with our friends, children, and grandchildren are irreplaceable. Remember the ideas we teach young people today will be with them when we are just memories.

The author and his father each holding a nice catch of smallmouth bass. Fishing is a sport that people can be involved in at all stages of their life.

Four generations of fishermen come together in this photo. The author with his father, his son, and his grandson display the day's catch.

CHAPTER 5

Seasons Of
The River

To be a successful river angler, one must develop an understanding of changes in the river as a result of seasons, whether it is just wet and dry seasons in a tropical river or in temperature climate the four seasons of the year. The movements of fish from shallow to deep areas as well as some actual migration may occur with certain species of fish. If you as a fisherman are searching for that species, you must have a good understanding of these movements.

Walleye would be a good species to cite as an example of this. During winter months they are usually found in very deep pools (deepest in the river) in large schools. As spring arrives, they spread out and may be found throughout the river in more shallow areas. In the Northeast rivers, the walleye will move back to the deep once again. In the fall on overcast days, a fisherman may find a school of walleye and catch a large number of them with minnows or jigs.

A very important thing to keep in mind is that the length of the seasons on each river varies as a result of the river's location as far as longitude is concerned, but altitude also has to be taken into consideration. In many cases the seasons are considered intently by the angler in his attempt to do other activities or hobbies. Fishermen who also hunt, snow ski, or simply those who only enjoy fishing in short sleeve shirts will put the fishing tackle away on Labor Day or shortly thereafter. However, if they fished at that time, they may find that fishing actually gets better possibly for two reasons. The first being that there is less human activity on the river, and the second is that many species of fish feed up before water temperatures drop excessively. Another point to keep in mind is some species become more active at lower water temperatures. Walleyes are a very good example of this.

In looking at the different seasons of the river, much emphasis must be placed on varying fishing techniques with river conditions at each season and also the angler must think about the species of fish that they are pursuing.

Temperature ranges at both ends of the spectrum may require the angler to fish much more slowly and at different times of the day. Examples of this would be the angler may want to fish during the heat of midday in the winter season and during the night hours in the summer season.

The angler who has just started to fish all of the seasons of his particular river will definitely have to experiment with times and techniques and not get discouraged with not catching fish on a certain fishing trip. If a certain time or technique doesn't produce, it may even be the wrong area of the river being fished. I have discovered in most cases in the winter months here in Pennsylvania that the deepest pools are more productive for walleyes and the occasional smallmouth.

The smallmouth will take the minnow only if it is almost in their mouth at the lower winter water temperatures. They will not chase the minnow as they do at other times of the year. On the other hand, walleyes will bite readily, and in areas of the river where other anglers don't know they are present.

On some southern rivers, the seasonal changes also provides time when fishing for certain species of game fish or pan fish becomes an expected ritual just as other activities and hobbies are seasonal. One must keep in mind that the fish life cycles and breeding seasons are tied to the seasons of the river, and certain times become a very high activity period for each species. Most of the river species are spring spawners, and they will move about in the river from late winter in preparation of the spawning time. This compares to the movement of species of fish to various water depths in large lakes.

The author with a catch of bass taken fishing from late evening to the next morning. Many smaller specimens released. The two day limit applies here in Pennsylvania. The smallest fish here was 16 inches and the largest 19 inches. All fish caught took minnows fished in a deep pool below a set of riffles.

This catch of smallmouth bass and a 31 inch musky was caught by the author and Brian Boyles. Brian caught the musky on a 3 inch native minnow. The smallmouth bass were from 15 to 19 inches in length.

CHAPTER 6

Times Not To Fish

There are times a fisherman would be better off staying home and doing chores that would be a problem for him at a later time. Many times a fisherman may have conflicts with a mate or another person for putting off chores of mowing grass, painting rooms, or a thousand other things. My friends and I have discovered that attempting to fish under certain conditions only creates frustration and a waste of time and possibly money.

The wise fisherman can tell very easily when these times are. The first to come to mind is right after a heavy storm or constant rain for several days, when the river is nearly at flood-stage and muddy. The inexperienced fisherman will try to find a place to fish and spend a lot of time searching for a back-water area where his line will be thrown up on shore as soon as he casts it into the water. In most cases the fish are not hungry from early feeding as the water rose and are just trying to avoid being swept downstream. Feeding is the least thing of concern for them. For several days after this period as the river level drops, fish are primarily making adjustment and feed very rarely and fishing during this period should be avoided unless one has taken vacation time from work and has very little other opportunities to fish.

A second time to avoid is a period of windy weather, usually as a result of atmospheric pressure changes. It seems as the surface winds approach 8-10 mph, the fish really turn off. I have found this type of weather can actually feel quite pleasant to the person fishing and yet be very unproductive as far as successful fishing is concerned.

The fish are really lethargic during this kind of weather, and even with extremely good bait and proper presentation, results leave a lot to be desired. I have attempted to fish under these conditions only because some of my fishing buddies have coaxed me into going with them as they have the day set aside from their work schedule in advance of the frontal system moving through.

I have yet to see a good catch of fish of any species on a day described above. Not only do you waste time and money fishing on a constantly windy day, but usually a waste of bait occurs also. It appears that small fish will feed, and it is really a downer to have small fish take bait that usually they cannot get near because of competition from larger ones.

Another time wasted is the early morning hours after a fair drop of air temperature during the night. This type of situation causes a fog to come off the surface of the river. I have yet to see much fish activity during this period. I never rush to fish the morning hours when this occurs. This is really a frequent happening in late summer and early fall on rivers from Virginia north in the East and in many of the larger rivers in the West depending upon the elevation.

It is much more advantageous for the fisherman to spend the early hours in bed and leave for the river at a time that will get them fishing about 8-10 am. Even species of fish that feed a lot at night will quit earlier during these types of situations. Spending the actual productive hours fishing will provide more pleasure and allow the other hours for rest and getting personal chores out of the way.

Weekends and heavy holiday times are also good to avoid, if at all possible, because so much activity may be going on that the fish are too frightened to feed. If one is limited in the days one can fish, the odd hours of extremely early morning or during the night may be productive if the weather conditions cooperate.

The quiet times are taken advantage of by fish and they will feed. If the fishermen also take advantage of these hours, they may catch some extremely good fish as well as enjoy the quiet and solitude of being somewhat alone from the bustle of boats, water skiers and amateur fishermen. It definitely is not relaxing or productive when the water is sloshing back and forth on the river banks as if it was a bathtub.

It is actually amusing just watching people trying to fish under these conditions. It can be extremely frustrating if you try and think you can do well at this time. The fish are most likely lying on the bottom of the deepest pools beside a big rock just riding out the hectic time. Definitely feeding on anything thrown past them is ignored unless they are small and not able to feed at other times because of the competition. If you are on vacation at this time, instead of fishing during the high activity time, either join the boaters, spend time with the wife and kids, or if alone, catch a nap or read a good book.

If this is an area of a river you are not familiar with, this is a really good time to explore and learn where good looking areas of the river are for later reference. In states that have opening days of fishing for certain species of fish—trout, bass, or others, the river traffic may also reach a level where fishing is almost a waste of time.

It is much more productive to simply explore the river and

look for changes that have occurred from winter storms, hurricanes or man's construction of bridges. So many river fishermen have caught the same disease that lake fishermen have—the obsession with speed and power. They get powerboats or air boats and speed from place to place on the river, stopping occasionally to cast a line or bait and after 10 minutes or so in an area, they rip off to a new location.

Another situation that involves proper timing are areas of rivers affected by tidal surges. Even areas upriver from the salt water or mixed salt and freshwater, called brackish water, are affected in flow and depth. Fish have adapted their feeding schedules to match these periodic changes. I have found the best time to fish is when the tide is coming in. It appears as if the bait fish and fishbait are more exposed to the feeding fish at this time. The slack periods also seems productive, but as the tide surge leaves, fishing almost always is quite poor. You can get tidal tables from newspapers or bait and tackle stores if the need arises.

Many rivers have electric generating dams which also alter the flow and level of rivers, and they can be extremely difficult to fish because of this. In most cases this generation is done on a schedule that can be found out by contacting the power company or the people responsible at the generating site. Once again it seems as if the fish really turn off as the river rises. I believe the fish feed in rhythm to the water, adapt to this and just turn on and off. If a fisherman gets the generating schedule, he can adjust to this just as a tidal schedule.

During a drought time, a river fisherman can get in some very productive fishing between power producing time below dams. The fish get concentrated in the deeper pools, and if the fisherman fishes slowly and quietly, he can catch a lot of trophy-sized fish. This is a time when conservation is very important.

It would be very easy at this point to overfish the stream. Catch and release is a very important concept. One must also look at the number of individual species and realize that it may be necessary to harvest certain species in relatively large amounts and some large fish of almost all species represented. It must be kept in mind that the reduced water area has less food, oxygen, and living space. The fishing public at large does not clearly understand the significance of constantly releasing certain species of fish and keeping game fish. In many cases certain fish are just as good in the pan as the more highly publicized game fish.

Sometimes the introduction of a new species into a watershed can be extremely harmful. An example of this is the introduction of striped bass into manmade lakes. Other species suffer as a result of this. Largemouth bass populations usually drop where stripers are introduced. Tourist money and fishing tournaments may be responsible for this type of project. The striped bass are almost worthless in the pan and have to be constantly stocked as they do not reproduce in manmade fresh water lakes. It is not my goal or desire to put down stocking programs, and I will be the first to admit I don't know everything about a particular watershed.

CHAPTER 7

Rivers I
Have Fished

Since the industrial revolution, many of our rivers have turned into open sewers with tremendous amounts of industrial waste in addition to city sewage. Recently we have seen a swing toward concern for our water, and there are many different federal and state programs to clean up the environment.

In addition to this attitude, the closing of a lot of our industrial base has reversed the process of pollution.

Just as a farm which is no longer farmed reverts back to forest or prairie, so does a river eventually heal itself unless the pollution is an extremely dangerous chemical such as kepone or heavy metals. In some cases government wants to take credit for the process, but much can be said about the industrial closings and cleaner rivers.

As a river improves in water quality, many of the support organisms for fish start to populate the stream. Eventually stonefly, dobsonfly, and mayfly larva can survive, and then crayfish, minnows, and larger fish come down out of the feeder streams.

The rejuvenation process slowly continues until discovered by a fisherman. After a period of time, the river becomes a bonanza for fishermen until the time occurs when the fishing pressure is greater than the stream can handle. Similar situations to this are occurring all around the country. Fishing pressure is crippling many rivers to the point of long-lasting damage.

In Pennsylvania we have had several rivers go through this transition from being a polluted eyesore to a recreational paradise and then to an over-fished resource. A real good example of this is the Little Juniata River from Tyrone to the confluence with the Frankstown branch of the same river. Volunteer brown trout moved into the river after sewage treatment improved, and the local industries stopped placing raw industrial waste into the stream. Fishermen soon discovered the wild trout population and started fishing the river heavily.

The introduction of thousands of brown trout fingerlings has not helped keep the population up because the size limit was left to seven inches. The stream would have been better served by putting a 15 or 20 inch trophy size on that section and kept the number of fish permitted to one per day. It is now just a stream with a lot of available crayfish, minnows and trash fish such as fallfish. The stream is still touted as good fishing, but anglers who fish it tell me the large native browns are not there in good numbers any longer. In all fairness to the fish commission, it is a very difficult job balancing the forces they have to deal with. The entire Juniata river system is being fished more heavily each season, and more and more fishing tournaments are being held.

It is good to have such resources available, but recently the legal size limit for bass was raised to 12 inches and 6 per day. The Susquehanna and its other tributaries also have this limit down to the state capital at Harrisburg, and below that the bass have to be 15 inches. It may be that this size limit will have to be extended to the entire watershed. I have fished similar rivers that had a slot system and this could be investigated. The last couple of paragraphs are included just to give the reader an idea of what can happen to a river system as the water quality improves and fishing pressure increases.

In this chapter I want to discuss some river systems I have visited and fished and point out similarities and differences as a result of fishing for different species of fish and also different river sizes, ages, and the results of faster or slower fall of elevation. I also want to emphasize that minnow fishing has worked for me in all of these outings.

As one travels throughout the country, several things must always be checked out. I always attempt to find out what the poisonous snake situation is along the river I intend to fish. Keep in mind river fishing is, in most cases, in the more remote areas and snakes can be a real problem. My son Lance and I have had encounters with copperheads, water moccasins, and even a wild alligator. Rivers that have moccasins along it should not be waded. This is where the jon boat comes in handy. The advantages of a jon boat are lightness, stability, and shallow draft which is perfect for most rivers. We do have a five horsepower kicker for it but prefer to row or pole our way into fishing areas.

Other problems you may come across are large numbers of mosquitoes, ticks, and spiders. Along the river banks most rivers in the East have extremely large amounts of poison ivy, which can be quite a problem if you are allergic. One word to the wise here, you can react to poison ivy at any time even though you have been around it for years and never had a case. It is also a yearround problem; even in winter in northern states if you touch the stems or roots you may get a reaction. And if you accidentally burn the plant in a camp fire, even your eyes may swell shut. I have known cases of wives getting poison ivy from handling the husbands fishing gear. As I always tell my friends, be careful out there and learn to recognize the hazards you may encounter.

Another suggestion is to get yourself a good life vest (coast guard approved) and wear it. After considering all of that, if you still are interested in river fishing, you are on your way to a lot of fun. Because of the large number of lakes and impoundments in some states, the rivers have very little fishing pressure. North Carolina is a very good example of this, and in a two year period while my son was at Fort Bragg, we caught a lot of nice fish particularly some very nice channel catfish and largemouth bass. I would like to describe some rivers we fished there so you can get the idea of how you can go to a strange area and use the methods to get good fishing.

The Roanoke River in northeastern North Carolina was a river that gave us much delight. Three of us had gone to an area near the town of Williamston to hunt the Roanoke wetlands for deer with muzzleloaders. We discovered not only did we get into good deer hunting, but we got in some really good fishing for channel cats. We had to use the jon boat to get back into the wetlands area to hunt.

After the first trip into the hunting area, we decided the middle hours of the day may be used more productively by fishing rather than on the deer stands in the swamp. We used an umbrella net to catch some minnows in a small feeder stream and then kept them in the river in metal minnow buckets with holes for the water to move through. We had to travel about two miles up river to our hunting area and would go up while it was still dark.

After hunting till about 10 am, we slowly worked our way out and located several good catfish holes with deepwater and fallen logs. We caught many good channel catfish in the 25 to 30 inch range. They really put up good battles and provided good filets for deep frying back at the travel trailer at a local campground.

My wife and I use a Fry Pappy and a special batter mix that a friend of ours, Columbus George, has given us. It provides a golden brown coat that simply makes the fish we cook delicious. It does not become saturated with oil, and we always use canola oil to deep fry our fish. This trip was simply a double winner because of the fish caught along with our successful deer hunting.

The Roanoke River in the area mentioned is a mature river, slow moving and and having deep pools. The problem a fisherman may have here is being able to distinguish the deep pools from the long slow runs. The slow runs have only smaller channel cats and pan fish. The river does have current in it, and it appears to be slower moving than it actually is.

The terminal tackle used in fishing here was one or two hooks above a small sinker I call an egg sinker. The minnows were hooked either through the back or through the tail. The hooks were tied on leader and then tied to a swivel. The sinker was tied to lighter line (4 lb. test) and then to the swivel. If the sinker gets caught on a log or something, the light line would break and only the sinker would be lost. The minnows would be up the line about 15 inches; this would keep them off the bottom. Catfish will pick minnows up more easily that way because of the shape of their mouths.

Another trip to North Carolina took us across the state to the western mountains and a totally different river setting, The French Broad River. My son Lance had been to the Asheville area with a group from the army on a whitewater rafting trip and was quite impressed with the river. He described it to me and I decided I had to fish it.

We traveled to Hot Springs, a small community along the river near the Tennessee border. The river has an extremely steep gradient, as you probably realized when I mentioned whitewater rafting. It has a lot colder water temperature than you would expect in North Carolina but the mountains are over 4,000 feet in elevation. In fact the upper reaches of the river support trout.

The area down closer to Hot Springs supports channel catfish and smallmouth bass. The French Broad River makes one think of a river farther north because of the nature of the fishbait and baitfish. We caught hellgramites and crayfish and lots of minnows to use for fishing. The French Broad River has very easily identified riffle, pool, and run characteristics because of its steep grade.

One can wade this river if you do it very carefully, and I would emphasize that it should never be done without a good life vest. It is fished very little and mostly by local people for the decent channel cats present in the river. We caught mostly 4-5 pounders, but I saw pictures in one bait shop of some 30 lb. fish. Smallmouth fishing is not intentional and rarely mentioned. I feel a record-sized trophy is possible here. The only setback to this possibility is a fish kill a few years back from some industrial spill.

It is a beautiful river with extremely wild areas. We did come into contact with a couple of copperheads, and the area looks like real rattlesnake country. If a fisherman keeps this in mind, The French Broad River could be a great place to spend some fishing time. Do not attempt to use any boats on this river as it is primarily rafting, and a solid boat or canoe would simply get smashed on the rocks. There are some real falls on sections of the river. Another thing to be concerned about is rapid water rise in heavy rain times. With the steep mountains, the river will rise to floodstage quickly.

A very small river which is interesting to fish in North Carolina is the Deep River. The Deep River is a slow moving river with not much of a gradient so it is difficult to read as to where the actual pools are located. So much of a river of this nature is relatively nonproductive that many fishermen give up. My son Lance and I fished it one time in early May and caught several burlap bags full of catfish. We got into several pools that produced a catfish with every cast of a minnow.

Lance and I fished several rivers in Texas with similar success for catfish, largemouth bass, and white bass, which are called sand bass by many local people.

The point I am trying to make is the techniques I have talked about in this book will work on any river if time is taken to study the river and its feeder streams. If a fisherman can link up with a resident riverman, it is much easier, but sometimes even they can learn some fresh techniques from a traveling riverman. The traveling angler can learn a lot about an area by keeping his ears open at gatherings of extended family, church socials and meetings of that nature.

Just to reinforce what I said before, one must be friendly and a good listener to stories and be able to ask questions without appearing to be too inquisitive about someone's favorite fishing pools. The angler should try to ask questions also about how live minnows are obtained in the area. If the locals are talking about using minnows from the local bait store, they probably are not real dedicated river fishermen even though they may provide important information of where to start exploring a local river. Dedicated river fishermen will refuse to buy bait for two main reasons. One is cost, but the major reason is they don't feel the shiners or fathead minnows sold in bait stores will do well as bait for river fish. Both of the mentioned baitfish are primarily lake raised and are not hardy enough for river fishing. The large old fish in the river will probably not give that type of bait a second glance. Naturally occurring minnows in the watershed are much more accepted and provide the angler with a free plus hardier bait. Nothing is worse than getting to where you are going to fish and find that all of your shiners are in the minnow bucket belly up. At three dollars a dozen, that can be the beginning of a bad day.

There may be certain techniques of catching local minnows that are not real familiar to you, but spend some time finding out how the locals get their bait. You will be just as successful after a few tries.

Good places to fish are where there are deep areas above the rocks at the end of the run, plus many deep pockets around rocks in the riffles. In addition, below the riffles is a deep pool where many trophy-sized fish are there for the taking.

The same riffle shown above from a different angle. Notice that below the riffle is a pool that contains pillars from a railroad bridge. This type of area is always productive with live minnows, if the water level and temperatures cooperate.

CHAPTER 8

Fisherman Sense – Fish Senses

This is a chapter of unequaled importance in fishing rivers successfully. Any person who wants to be a good outdoorsman studies his quarry. A white tail deer hunter or turkey hunter spends years studying and learning about the wildlife they hunt, but most fishermen believe that throwing attractive hardware in a river will have game fish fighting each other to get caught.

A couple of things always amaze me. First, how do anglers think fish get to be lunkers if they strike every piece of flashing hardware thrown their way. Secondly, it appears as if every fisherman thinks all other anglers can't present the lure the way they do. This second point does have some validity because I know a family of trout fishermen who are extremely successful using only spinners as their terminal tackle. They also practice many other of the suggestions I have made in the previous chapters.

Now let me look at the senses that a fish has and how it uses those senses to stay alive. Remember the whitetail and all of its tricks and the acute senses it uses to avoid most hunters. Large trophy fish in public waters are just as wary and use all of their senses.

There is no question that sight in fish is a very important

sense to identify danger and also food. A fish can recognize by sight the food that it consumes on a daily basis. I know some fish strike some unusual items occasionally, and in some cases this may be a result of protecting a spawning bed or territory.

I do not want to depend upon an occasional strike. It is my desire to catch big as well as large numbers of fish each trip out. Giving fish a sight they recognize as a common meal to them will provide a larger numbers of bites than anything else. It is also apparent that fish recognize the common food items in that section of stream in which they reside. If the bait or lure is unnatural looking, I doubt that the lunkers jump at this opportunity to feed.

The fish also sees other things you as an angler may not want seen, such as the hook. I always wonder why fishermen want to use gold hooks. In fact I put my hooks in water and then dry them out so they develop a very thin coat of rust on them. This does not affect their sharpness. It just stops any glare they may have. Brass swivels and such may be a problem. Other fishermen besides me are concerned about the fish seeing the line.

Many anglers don't take into consideration that the fish may have seen them and go into hiding. Dark clothing may help with this but being careful where you stand and how close you get to the area being fished are more important. Wading right into the area to be fished or floating a boat right over the area being fished should be a obvious no-no, but I see it all the time. I realize we consider ourselves the most intelligent animal on earth, but does that mean everything else including gamefish is totally stupid?

The second fish sense to consider is hearing. Fish live in a terrific medium for transmission of sound—water. If you don't think sound travels well in water, put your head under and let a friend pound two rocks together under the surface. Actually that could be bad for your ears so please just take my word for it, that sound travels well in water. Fish have good receptors for sound, and the lateral line the whole length of their body picks up low frequency noises.

This hearing gives the fish warning about possible predators in the water as well as large land carnivores like bears. Fish do get used to certain sounds such as train sounds or highway sounds if those occur close to a river. The sound of water splashing and noise in the water itself means that danger can be near. This isn't really a problem with nursery stocked trout as it is with wild ones or members of other species of fish.

Waters that are heavily fished have fish that survive by being in tune with the sound around them. I avoid moving quickly and stirring or splashing water. One must remember in public water in highly populated areas most fish have been caught several times in their lives before they reach legal size or for some species large enough to be kept for the pan. Fish that don't become wary don't live long.

Fish, either by instinct or by learning, recognized normal river sounds and whatever sounds their food sources may make. I don't have any idea, other than fluttering and splashing, what sounds a minnow may make. I tend to believe many noises are not made by a crawfish or any other fresh bait that would be made naturally to attract a feeding fish. It makes me wonder why some people believe whirling noise and sonar vibrations would attract feeding fish.

Probably most anglers do not think much of the combined senses of taste and smell. In water it is difficult to separate taste from smell, but the important thing to keep in mind is fish respond to smell quite accurately. Many fish can feed as well at night or in cloudy water as during the day and smell has to be used for this.

Almost all anglers are aware of catfish having sensitive smelling apparatus, but all game fish can smell and then taste their prey with great accuracy. This is definitely a plus for bait fishermen, but it also can be a problem if something does not smell right.

I have had occasions when fishing companions would have insect repellents or sunscreen on their hands, and even though they were using the same type and size minnows, would not catch fish and I would. I always avoid having anything on my hands that will get on my line, hooks, or bait. I won't even change oil in my car or truck the day before I go fishing. I fill my gas tank the day before because it is difficult to avoid getting some gasoline on your hands.

I read a study somewhere how small amounts of gasoline would be avoided by fish. I am sure they don't want anything like that on their food. It is annoying to me when I mention this to fishermen and they act as if I am out of my mind, but then during hunting season they will spend all kind of time and money to avoid having their scent get on the ground near their deer stand.

It is my contention that the fish can recognize the smell of different minnows, crayfish, and hellgramites that live in the water shed. It could well be that the older, larger fish have learned to avoid strange smells in the water.

I do feel that smaller fish also sense when larger predators such as muskies are feeding. Sometimes when I fish a pool that usually produces a large number of middle-sized fish and it appears to be empty of life, I get the feeling that a big bad guy is on the prowl. Even a 15 inch smallmouth would avoid a hungry musky in the 40 inch range.

Touch is probably the least of the senses, and yet fish use this in mouthing their food. Many fish have barbels near their mouth for touching, but it is my belief all fish can tell by touch whether the food is natural or not.

During the fall months in the northern rivers, many fish will simply stop the bait such as a minnow and just lie there with it and then swallow it without actually taking any line. This is probably where touch plays a very important part of feeding. In the fall months of September and October, I am aware of how these fish react. One week I was fishing a pool with minnows and had a 20 inch walleye just stop the minnow and swallow it. Realizing that this is common for this time of year I usually watch for my line to stop its normal drift, and many times it is just caught, and I have to get it lose or break it off.

What I do is slowly raise the rod tip and slowly reel in the slack line. An angler can feel the fish and this is the time to set the hook. If the fish feels the line drag and the fisherman does not set the hook right away, the fish will spit out the minnow. They actually just blow out the bait. Many people do not even know they have a fish biting. Experiences such as this will be gained over time for your river and the species of fish that you are angling for.

Many times as I fish, I wonder if members of the same species have any communication. If this is possible, I wonder what happens when small fish are released. Keep in mind many fish are schooling fish and they are constantly together. A fish may telegraph just by its actions fear to other fish in the school, just as the actions of a scared doe may warn a buck deer. It is my feeling that whatever the fisherman can do to improve his fishing should be considered. I even avoid eating certain foods such as onions or garlic food that may be transmitted thru the pores of my hands onto my fishing tackle and bait.

The author with a 10 lb. channel cat caught on a 7 inch sucker. The fish was given lots of time to swallow the bait and made two runs before the hook was set.

A very nice catch of bass caught by Bill Schirf and the author one day in August. The fish were from 14 to 18 inches in size. This day the actual catch of legal bass for both anglers was 78. All except those in the picture were carefully returned.

CHAPTER 9

Keeping
Records Of
Your Catches

This is not my idea originally, but the reader will recall my mention of the family that probably catches more native trout than anyone else in the State of Pennsylvania. I got the idea of keeping records from this family. There are several reasons to keep records. One is it gives you a clear understanding of the weather and river conditions when you were highly successful. Secondly, they also tell you what the water conditions and temperatures were during that time.

Another point to keep in mind is they provide you with a written account that is much better than memory of exactly where, when, and how you caught these fish. An example of how important this can be is how I use the information to judge the present season with years past. I can then determine if certain areas of a river should be allowed to rest and new fishing areas found. Don't fish an area to such low levels of fish that it will take a long time to recover, keeping in mind that natural reproduction is the key here.

The records also have pointed out the best times to fish both on a daily basis and what parts of the season are most productive. Many people wonder why I am in no hurry to go fishing early in the morning. It is a result of records showing that early morning is the least productive time to fish, especially in the fall.

When many fishermen are out there during the early part of the season pounding the water with high expectations, I rarely spend much time fishing. I don't even get excited until after the 4th of July on the local rivers. If I go south, I find that in North Carolina on the Cape Fear or the Deep River late April and early May are really good for channel catfish, bass and large brim. The summer months are very slack and fishing some places is quite slow. If you keep records, you know these things and thus plan accordingly.

During the first couple of weeks, bass fishing the rivers of Pennsylvania is almost a waste of time. I go to get a feel for the river. Even though there are lots of fishermen out there, it is the river conditions that appear to cause the fishing to be slow. In the case of smallmouth bass, the fish have just completed spawning and may be moving about or simply not feeding much at this time. Even good minnows presented properly do not attract many strikes.

With smallmouth bass I only record information on bass over 12 inches long. I record the location where the fish was caught, the day of the month, and time of day. I write into the account a note concerning the weather, air temperatures, water temperature, and water level. Any unusual circumstance is also placed in the record. If I keep the fish, I also check the stomach contents. I add a note about this in my notebook to see if there is anything special about the feeding of fish in that particular section of river.

Every article I have read about smallmouth bass fishing is how important crayfish are as a food source and as bait. This is a result of analysis of stomach contents. However, in my opinion this is because crayfish can easily be caught by bass, channel cats, and trout particularly at night when all of the organisms just mentioned are active. It does not mean the game fish prefer crayfish. Game fish of almost all species will jump on a minnow, and yet when stomach contents are compared, crayfish are more numerous than minnows. This past season I checked the stomach contents of eight walleye from 18 to 27 inches long and one 10 lb. channel catfish. They all had crayfish, but all smacked sucker minnows of 4-5 inches in length.

Most articles written about walleyes stress using minnows or minnow-like lures, and yet the walleyes I caught contained crayfish. The reason is simply: the crayfish are numerous and easily caught and not their favorite food. I don't fish with crayfish unless I can't get minnows. If I run out of minnows, I sometimes catch a few crayfish and hellgramites to finish the day.

For several years I fell for the crayfish theory as being the best live bait for smallmouth bass and channel catfish. I believe after years of fishing many rivers throughout the country and keeping records of my catches that minnows are the best live bait for almost all species of game fish. The more you fish them the more sophisticated you get at presentation and hooking fish with them. It is apparent from my recorded results minnows will consistently produce fine catches.

The last point I want to emphasize is if the records show a trend of successful behaviors, go with them. Don't be afraid to change techniques and also don't be afraid to think differently than other fishermen. I know fishermen who spend hours at night catching soft shelled crayfish. I am not saying they don't catch some nice fish because I believe softshells have a particular odor that turns on fish but on a consistent basis minnows actually do better. I never argue with other fishermen. I just continue to fish, keep records, and pursue fish with a vengeance and the techniques that have worked for me.

The simplest things sometimes can make a difference. Sometimes just the addition of another splitshot can make an angler start catching fish. When you catch fish in a certain hole, record which side of the river you were fishing and any particular landmark or river rock you were close to upon catching a fine fish. I also note any large fish that I had on that snapped the line or got off. This can be significant the next time you approach the same fishing spot.

I realize all of this takes time, but it really does help you become more successful and helps you understand conditions that may make fishing a waste of time. One thing was quite evident after collecting several years of data: fishing tables on the calendar have very little value unless they motivate the angler; however, motivating the fish to bite is a totally different matter.

This is a nice catch of smallmouth bass caught by the author and his neighbor Fred Boyles an evening in September. The bass were from 14 to 18 inches in length. All were caught on native minnows.

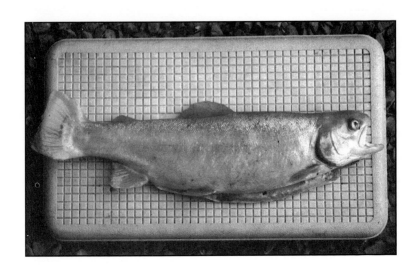

CHAPTER 10

When You Learn The Most

I do enjoy fishing with friends, but there is much to gain by spending some time alone along your fishing river. This is time when you learn the most about several things including yourself. Being alone is a special time when one can analyze the river, the living relationships of organisms in and around the river, and how you as a transgressor can be there with as little disruption as possible. It is a great time to watch the interaction between the river life.

During the many sessions I have had alone on the river, I have watched muskies feeding as well as other species. It is interesting to just be quiet and see what is stirring, sometimes chasing a school of minnows or a frog as it tries to reach an opposite shore. So many times a river fisherman can see the difference between the real life drama and what he attempts to create in his fishing methods.

The wildlife that interacts with the river and its inhabitants has also taught me a lot about the importance of being quiet and sneaky in my fishing. An example of this is to watch the wading birds such as the Great Blue Heron. So much of their time is spent standing still waiting for prey. Modern man has lost so much of his patience. The real successful hunters and fishermen I know are not in a hurry to get anywhere, such as from one boat launch to another down stream.

In watching nature one realizes it is necessary to develop a proper perspective of what we as anglers are trying to accomplish. It really is interesting to start the day quietly getting your bait and watching your surroundings. This gives the true river angler a calm time to address the needs of the inner self and begin his escape from the daily stress of modern life.

This also gives the angler time to develop a real philosophy of what fishing actually means to him as an individual. It is a time to practice methods mentioned earlier in this book. The angler can take time to fish slowly without creating any waves or noise. He can use the knowledge gained about the river and the kinds of fish he is trying to catch. It is also a time when one can examine the presentation of the bait, study the way in which the fish is caught, and appreciate the beauty of the fish he is catching.

Interesting enough, as soon as Labor Day is over, river traffic and recreation drops tremendously, and even the weekends may be peaceful enough to head to a favorite fishing spot. It is a time when many people are turning to the weekend football season and other outdoor people are going hunting. Early fall fishing may be successful for two reasons. One is that the fish are preparing for the long winter months; the other may be it's simply a quieter time, and the angler does not have to compete with all of the other human activity on the river.

An angler heading out alone should tell someone close to him where he is going and give that person a reasonable time to expect him home. It is with good judgement that the fisherman wears a good life vest and is more cautious of poisonous snakes and rocky areas in the river. A person should know his physical limitations and stay within them without exhausting himself.

Many of my successful fishing trips have been alone, and I feel this may be because when fishing by myself, I tend to move more slowly and practice being extremely quiet. Another point to remember even if your fishing friend has similar fishing habits, all his movements and noises are added to yours.

After Labor Day the river fisherman may want to concentrate his efforts on particularly deep pools in the river as fish start to prepare for winter. Certain species such as walleye and channel catfish will head for these deep pools to spend the colder months. Channel catfish may travel fairly large distances to get into the deeper holes. Smallmouth bass will not travel far and simply go into the deepest part of the riffle, pool, and run area they call home.

In rivers that have large brown trout that spend their summers staying in a spring fed area of the river, the fall is a high activity period. The river water cools and the big trout will go on a feeding frenzy. I have caught some nice brown trout where other fishermen would be shocked to find them.

The middle of the week, in most cases, is the best time to spend alone at your favorite fishing spot. It is a time when many of the inhabitants are finally able to spend some time without the noise, vibrations, and action from all the human activity.

The author fished alone one evening and caught these smallmouth on redfin minnows. The largest fish was 18 inches.

This October catch shows that as water temperature changes different species of fish may show up in the creel.

CHAPTER 11

Catching The Big Ones

There are two schools of fishermen besides lure and live bait people. There is the group that specializes in fishing for "average" sized fish using the lightest tackle available (ultra-lite), and the second group that goes after the "hawgs" of the lake or river. In this chapter I want to discuss fishing for the big guys. Most anglers say they want to catch big fish but then use bait and tackle best suited for "run of the mill" fish. This is not to say the average angler never catches large fish, but the person who specializes and has that goal foremost in his fishing techniques is the consistent one who catches the fish that make the newspaper.

In river fishing several things have to be considered. The first of these is will a particular stretch of water be a possible big fish producer. It seems as if several conditions are necessary for an area to be productive. River size is definitely a big factor. Big rivers have deep pools and sufficient food plus hiding places for large fish. A fisherman that angles for large fish is very species-oriented.

A person who specializes in catching large catfish, muskies, or trout is out to set records and prove himself as someone apart from the regular fisherman. No matter what species they are after, they have much more in common with each other than with other fishermen who fish for the same species. An angler who fishes a western river for huge brown trout has very similar techniques to an angler fishing for the big channel or blue cats in a southern river.

The largest members of most species of sport fish consumes large numbers of other fish including members of their own kind. I once caught a 23 inch brown trout with a partially digested 9 inch brown trout in its stomach. It still took the 5 inch sucker I caught it with.

In this book I constantly use the term minnow, but in actuality the bait may be a small bluegill, sucker, chub, perch or members of other species in specific areas of the country. In this part of Pennsylvania, striped bass fishermen buy small trout and use them as bait. The reason this is done is when the fish commission stocked Lake Raystown, they placed large numbers of fingerling trout in the lake as part of the stocking program. The stripers feed on these fingerlings and thus led to fishermen using trout as striper bait in this large body of water.

Throughout the country fishermen wanting to catch large fish in rivers fish the deep pools with large bait fish. Many of the serious big fish anglers I know spend a lot of night time hours fishing. They usually will let large suckers and chubs free swim with very little weight unless it is needed to get the bait down to the fish. These deep holes are where the big trout, catfish and bass hang out.

Any location where there is a dropoff into deep water will provide a hiding and feeding location for big fish. This is common knowledge among anglers. That is why there is so much fishing activity below the spillways of large dams. However, river fishermen should be aware that there is usually good holding spots at the ends on long runs. These areas are located right before the water drops over the next riffle. Big fish will hang out in these locations because any injured baitfish will be washed through this area as the river current picks up before the riffles.

The big fish angler uses specialized tackle. In many cases, in addition to larger reels with heavier line, the fishing rod is usually much stiffer to provide the hooking strength and resistance to the vicious fight the bigger fish put up. Many anglers that spend much time on the river have numerous stories of straightened hooks, snapped lines, and even broken rods as a result of hooking one of the big fish while using light and medium action rods.

The person fishing for big fish in most rivers uses at a minimum 15 lb. test line, and the guys after big blue and channel cats use 20-40 lb. test line.

This type of fishing requires a special talent. It means that the angler will spend a lot of night time away from home, and that surely is not going to over well with a non-fishing spouse. It also means that anglers who fish for only the really big fish with large minnows do not catch many fish. Some nights will pass without even one bite.

A friend of mine and I used to fish for large brown trout at night with bluegills as bait. We would catch several trout during the season, and most of them would be longer than 20 inches. We would also have many nights where it was difficult to stay awake because of no fishing activity. This does not mean that fishing is always that slow. I have had big fish hit my bait on the first cast. Patience is extremely important in this just as it is in turkey hunting.

In this type of fishing, having a good buddy who knows the river as well as you or better is a real plus, and all of the time spent on catching minnows and using the minnows goes much easier. Having a person to help you net the big fish is also really an advantage at night. It is difficult fighting a large fish during daylight hours. At night, obstacles and darkness work to the fish's advantage, and a helper gives an angler a chance to land that big trophy fish. This is a time a large long-handled boat net comes in handy no matter if you are on shore or on a boat. Many of my fishing attempts for big fish have been from large rocks that stick up in the river above dropoffs. I try to keep the use of bright lights to a minimum as I believe these lights will scare off the larger fish. Keep in mind these fish got big because they were aware of their surroundings.

Summer nights can be very pleasant but are also times when insects are quite active. Night anglers also have to keep in mind poisonous snakes move about at night.

Large fish will usually pick up the minnow and move off with it. This is not the time to attempt to hook the fish. A successful angler will let the fish have more time to swallow the bait. It may take several minutes after the initial run before the fish shows a second run. Once again patience is important. After missing a few fish, patience is easier learned. Many times the fisherman who pulls too soon will have the fish swim around as if it is hooked and then spit out the minnow and keep on going. This is a frustrating experience and gives the angler many hours of wishing for another chance.

Many of these large fish should be returned to the water after being carefully weighed and measured. The larger fish in many cases are not good eating and might as well be left to grow into larger trophies as well as give other anglers the opportunity to catch them. Extremely large fish in many watersheds are becoming quite rare, and a picture is just as good as a wall mount. I have attempted to eat large brown trout and have found they are strong tasting. Smaller fish are much better for the frying pan.

In situations where wild fish populations are doing well, a balance between that population and its environment is better served by taking certain sized fish for food. Fishing of any watershed can be overdone especially in areas of high human population. We all will see a lot of changes throughout the country, and even wild rivers will have to be watched carefully. Stocking programs do little but create "put and take" fishing. In wild trout rivers, restricting fishing methods is a poor approach, size and number limits work better.

This photograph shows a nice brown trout with several smallmouth bass caught out of a section of river where the transition is being made from trout water to a smallmouth stream. The trout is 19 inches and took a large native minnow. The bass were also caught on minnows and are between 14 and 15 inches in size.

A late October trip in the middle of the afternoon in the warm sun produced a channel catfish and two nice bass. The largest one is 19 inches. The fish take the minnows much more slowly this time of year in the northern part of the country.

CHAPTER 12

Researching Your Quarry

This chapter deals with discovering how, where, and when others successfully catch the fish you are in search of. A river fisherman usually has several species of fish he or she will come into contact with even though only one may be the actual quarry. Just recently, for example, a section of river I have been fishing for smallmouth has been extremely hot for walleyes for me and my fishing friends. We discovered this while fishing several of the deeper pools in early fall with redfin minnows. We caught quite a few walleyes in the two foot range. We were simply fishing minnows by bouncing them slowly along the bottom of the pool.

I have found I get a lot of information on recent good catches by checking state fishing magazines such as the Pennsylvania Angler. Most state fishing magazines will summarize the year's catches by a list of the citation fish of each species, where they were reportedly caught, when and what was used for bait or what lure was used; Pennsylvania has certain sizes and weight classes for each species for adult anglers and for youngsters.

I checked last year's channel catfish listed for both groups of anglers, and of one hundred large channel catfish, fifty three of them were said to have taken some form of minnow.

I always figure there is a certain number of people who don't give accurate data and information on where they actually caught a large fish. I know, for example, that a large musky was reported to have been caught on a local lake with a plug. A fishing acquaintance of mine told me the person caught the fish with a sucker in a deep pool on the same river I mentioned earlier.

The pool I mentioned in reference to the walleye is floated over constantly by anglers in boats and canoes. They throw lures and drift minnows through the holes, but the walleyes are holding right on the bottom. I have yet to find an angler who suspects this pool holds walleyes. I said they were deep pools, but that is a relative thing, and in the upper section of this river, a deep pool is only 6 or 7 feet deep. In shallow rivers I think boat noise is a real inhibitor to fish response. Angler presentation of bait or lure is not important if the fish are frightened.

In your early research, definitely some time should be spent visiting local bait stores looking for fish pictures and listening to the local anglers as they buy bait and tackle. In their excitement to get fishing, they will sometimes say things that will give you more information than if you ask direct questions. If you are from another area of the country, they will quickly pick up your dialect and possibly send you on a wild goose chase. Several times in my life I got information I knew from the start was to send me off to fish a place where the chance of catching a decent fish was less than winning a state lottery.

There are anglers who are friendly and want to help you as long as you don't go into their favorite section of the river and that I can understand. I give other anglers information about a river, but I don't tell them how to walk into my favorite pools.

In the bait shops, spend time looking at the tackle that is being sold and the line weight as well as hook sizes. See what types of bait are being sold and the variety of minnows and their sizes. I very rarely buy bait, but in a new area, after I get some idea of what is going on, I may buy some minnows until I explore how the natives catch them and where. I also try to find the pitfalls of the area. I don't wade in water that could have water moccasins swimming in it. I realize most people can't tell a poisonous snake from a non-poisonous one and label any water snake as a water moccasin. A word to the wise should be sufficient. Be careful out there and you will avoid injury and possibly even death.

In your exploration of a river, keep in mind that much of a river may produce good size fish, and it is important to be able to read water so you don't waste a lot of time fishing those areas. If you move into a new area, you may learn a lot from neighbors and fellow workers at your place of occupation. As people learn about you and become acquainted with you, they will eventually provide information and also help you link up with a real riverman. Many people fish rivers, but every area has a few real rivermen that know the local river like most people know their own home. You will find out who they are by just talking to them. To a riverman a river is one of his best friends, and he will talk about it in ways that only another river person will understand.

Once a true riverman recognizes you as kin, he will be very helpful, and over a period of time, if you become true friends, he will take you to some of his favorite pools and runs. He is trusting you not to exploit these places or to give out information to every Tom, Dick, or Harry. If you do, you will get no more from this person, and he will more likely not even speak to you. There is nothing more likely to build real friendship between you and this riverman than being able to keep these special places secret. One thing to keep in mind is that he has spent many hours to learn these places and he gave the knowledge as a sign of acceptance and friendship. I suggest that you carefully protect his special places. The riverman won't mind if you have a visiting relative along on a fishing trip, but he doesn't want these pools to become heavily fished.

The biggest suggestion I can give a river angler who has had to relocate is pay attention, listen, and talk very little. Even if you think you know more about rivers than the person doing the talking, you can learn much about a particular river system. Remember that even in periods of high inflation, know-it-alls are a dime a dozen.

The tradition of enjoying the outdoors passes from generation to generation. Teaching respect for and the care of our environment is a great part of this.

CHAPTER 13

Attributes Of Success For The Riverman

The measure of success can take many forms. The river angler may feel quite successful if he had a quiet day on the river. I am referring to the fisherman's success in catching fish. When I fish with others I find certain anglers almost always catch fish unless river conditions are hopeless.

I have watched my fishing friend George fish a section of water that others have just gone through without catching any fish, and he will catch several nice fish. He definitely has a certain knack in presentation and possibly the bait he is using is more suited to fish. I will say George is not as prone to stick to a certain bait as I am with minnows. George really likes to use softshell crayfish for bass and channel cats. The major attribute he has however besides his skill, is his patience. He even loses track of time and is late for many meals due to being in tune with the river.

If you believe the main thrust of your fishing day is to get from point A to point B, then fishing is not your main goal. From my experience it seems river fish are slow and patient feeders. They can pass up something that doesn't look right because the current will wash something else along.

Just like land predators that feed on the slow, weak, and sick animals, the river predators catch the weak that are washed to them by the flowing water. A predator does not have to strike quickly but can take the time to check the prey and reject what it doesn't want.

The angler needs to fish slowly and be extremely patient. I believe this is the main reason for success of river fishermen who fish with jigs slowly bouncing them along the bottom. Jig fishing and bait fishing are similar in much of the techniques of presentation.

Successful hunters and river fishermen are much alike in that they realize their quarry cannot tell time and does not worry that they must feed at a certain time. People have become so time-oriented that we let time govern almost all of our activities.

Sometimes just watching others in their movements on the river amuses me more than any antic done by a wild animal. Tournaments are so keyed to time that they rush from location to location making several cast of their lures and then onto a new place which they hope will provide the winning catch. After doing this for a period of time, the anglers really have lost the main reasons for being out on the lake or river. This is not a putdown, simply an observation of human nature. A close fishing buddy of mine was into the tournament scene and really was discouraged about fishing until he joined me and my slow pace on the river.

The four most important personal characteristics a successful river fisherman must have are alertness, stamina, patience, and more patience. An alert fisherman is aware of all his surroundings. He is aware of what the weather and water situations are and keeps on the lookout for dangers as well as what is occurring that will enable him to catch fish. The most important personal characteristic is the love that the river fisherman has for his favorite river.

A true river angler has such a deep commitment to and concern for the river that others cannot understand his feelings.

A good rocky area with small deep pockets where decent-sized gamefish and panfish such as rock bass can be easily caught.

Early October produces lower numbers of fish but sometimes some special catches. This picture shows a 24 inch walleye and a decent walleye caught on native minnows.

Selecting
Fishing
Companions

Other than being trapped into fishing with a marriage part-
ner, one can be selective with whom he or she fishes. Even if
you are fishing with children or grandchildren, one can train
them properly or simply not fish with them.

As much time as I spend on the river, I only fish with a few
close friends. Many people confuse acquaintances and
friends. My theory is an acquaintanceship is a more casual
relationship which occurs only because of a common work-
place or social membership and is not really or necessarily
based on similar concepts of how the outdoors is to be treat-
ed. So many times acquaintances that attempt to fish or hunt
together find they really have no common ground on which
to enjoy each others' company.

In today's world there is so much emphasis placed on male
bonding, whatever that means, but I have discovered that the
people I enjoy hunting and fishing with are most like me in
that they are loners who want to be in tune with nature more
than making an effort to get along with someone. In the cases
where I have developed close fishing companion- ships, it is
because of a similar interest in being deeply immersed in the
flow of nature, and conversation is mostly left to our travel
time to and from the river.

It is a pleasure to be able to teach youngsters the importance of enjoying the solitude and peace of the river and the wildlife around it. To be able to instruct a young family member or friend how all the plants, animals, and the river itself, depend upon man's protection and wise use makes one feel successful. A real outdoors person values all he comes in contact with. So much of human society is based upon self-gratification, no matter the cost to others or the environment. It is important that river fishermen instill in youngsters the need to protect, as much as possible, rivers and keep them as natural as we can in our heavily-populated world.

The river fisherman takes time to observe his natural setting and values each special place on the river he fishes.

So many times as we battle the bass, walleye, catfish or muskie, we become engrossed in the contest, but at other times our mind is free to listen, see, and ponder the wonderful world of the flowing river and appreciate everything surrounding us. It is important for our very being that this is never lost.

I realize this chapter is more of a philosophical statement than an instructional essay on how to catch the largest fish in a particular river, but I believe as you fish the river more years, you will actually blend yourself into your surroundings and get to feel as if you are actually a part of the place rather than a visiting stranger. This is how a true river fisherman is different from those that just fish the river.

CHAPTER 15

Battles Lost

Many times in fishing the river, an angler has an episode he remembers for a long, long time. It may be when he has caught a real trophy, or it may be when he has for one reason or another lost an exceptional fish. If the fisherman gets to see the fish making a jump or flashing in the water near him, that scene always remains vividly in his mind.

Fishermen, almost without exception, have experienced fish getting off the line, and each individual angler tries to reason out the cause of why he lost the fish. In many instances the loss of a fish can be attributed to the type of, or condition of, the tackle the fisherman was using. An angler cannot go to the river with old weakened line on his reel and expect to land big fish. Fishermen should keep their rods and reels well-maintained to prevent fish from getting off because of tackle not operating properly.

Getting the reel drag set properly is a very important skill that every angler must learn how to accomplish. The fish must be able to take line without snapping it. The angler can use a set of special scales designed for setting the pull against the drag, or he may guess how much stress the line is able to take. In most cases a fisherman can experiment with this by tying the end of his line to something solid, then testing the pull by how much effort is needed to make the drag release line from the spool.

In a certain number of cases, the tackle being used is simply not heavy enough to do the job. In river fishing an angler never knows when he is going to hook a fish that is too much fish for the tackle being used. In my own experiences, I have several occurrences when fish have taken all of the line from my reel without me even seeing the fish. I do remember one smallmouth bass that I lost.

My son Lance and I were fishing a pool, and I had a run on a large minnow. I hooked the fish and it came straight at me. Lance was downriver a short distance from me, and the smallmouth jumped approximately forty feet from both of us. It then turned down river and fighting the drag took all of my line. This was definitely a case of tackle too light for the job.

George and I were fishing a deep hole below a riffle on a medium-sized river. He cast a large minnow into the pool, and a fish immediately picked it up and made a run. George hooked the fish, and from the beginning it was obvious it was a large fish. His reel was broken and the drag did not work properly. The fish broke the 12 lb. test line and disappeared. This situation is a clear example of what can happen when tackle is not working properly. This is an example of why a fisherman should carry an extra rod and reel in his vehicle.

A third situation of loss of a trophy fish occurred when Bill and I were fishing a deep hole on a large river. Bill was fishing with a sucker approximately 6 inches in length. He had a fish pick it up and make a long run, and because of the size of the bait, he let the fish make a second run. Bill hooked the fish and it immediately jumped out of the water. I was watching and I told him it was a huge smallmouth bass.

The next situation that happened was a surprise. The fish swam right at Bill and he reeled in line as fast as he could to prevent slack line which most anglers would do to prevent the fish from getting off the line. The next thing that happened was the bass again jumped and was no more than 10 feet away. It made a rapid run and snapped the line. This fish was the largest smallmouth I have ever seen.

This fish loss was the result of a mistake made because neither Bill or I realized the best way of preventing what happened was to let some slack line so the fish would get away from us. The reel's drag was set properly, but the huge bass was so close that it overwhelmed the drag. This is a case where 20/20 hindsight comes into play. Even so the fish is still gone.

I cited these examples so that you can see the need for keeping your tackle in good shape, but also so that you can see that mistakes are made, and that fishing is more a challenge because some big ones get away.

CHAPTER 16

Accessories For River Fishing

In getting ready to fish rivers, it is good to plan your fishing strategy and then decide your necessities. If you are a beginner and lucky enough to hook up with a real riverman, he will help you in gathering the items you will need for your special river.

I am going to provide a list of what I find important in and on my river journeys. I will point out items that I feel you may need as extra backups to carry in your vehicle as I carry in my truck.

(A) Fishing rods, light or medium action with reels. I usually have 10 lb. test line on the spools. It may be good to carry extra spools with different weight lines.

(B) Fishing shoulder bag, containing the following items.

  1. Split shot containers, various size shot.

  2. Loose hooks in sizes 8, 6, 4, and 2. I keep hooks in plastic empty vitamin bottles that are water proof. These work better than hook containers sold at bait shops.

  3. Small container of swivels.

  4. Fish stringer.

  5. Forceps for removing hooks.

  6. A small water proof flashlight.

(C) Fine mesh landing net.

(D) Stainless steel pocket knife.

(E) 1. Pair of high top sneakers that are large enough. A half size larger than you normally wear works very well.

2. Pair of old slacks and a dark colored T-shirt. I suggested slacks instead of blue jeans as they can become quite irritating when they are water-soaked.

3. Wide brim hat to prevent sunburn and possibly skin cancer.

(F) A metal minnow bucket with holes in it to keep the minnows in the river. The bucket should be labeled with name, address and fishing license number. The bucket has an outer container for moving from one pool to another.

(G) A small bait container you can attach to your belt or hang by a nylon rope in case you need to catch hellgramites and crayfish.

This second part of the list are items you use or may need that are kept in your vehicle.

(A) An extra light or medium action rod and reel spooled with 10 lb. test line.

(B) Extra spool of 6 lb. test line in case the water level is extremely low and clear.

(C) Change of clothes to wear home.

(D) Hip boots and minnow seine.

(E) Styrofoam minnow buckets.

(F) Extra tackle in case you lose some in the river. It may be advantageous to have equipment for night fishing such as a good lantern.

(G) A good cooler with drinks, lunch and plastic bags to keep fish, in case you decide to keep some for the pan.

If the situation is such that seining minnows is out for various reasons, then the angler should have an umbrella net or a minnow trap. The type of habitat you are faced with will determine what will work best.

As a last resort, I will purchase minnows. I find that most bait shops have shiners or other lake minnows that are not very hardy and are best used for lake or pond fishing.

The only time I keep any dead minnows is if I am fishing for channel catfish after dark. I will then take the dead ones and smash them a little so the fish smell spreads through the water. This will attract channel catfish, eels, and also snapping turtles.

CHAPTER 17

Fighting Fish –
It's A Reel Drag

An angler can identify a person as a beginning fisherman quickly if he watches the angler attempt to land fish.

As an angler gains experience, he realizes that the rod and reel are more then a lever by which a fish is lifted from the water. An experienced fisherman understands modern tackle is designed to play a fish and exhaust it if the angler uses it carefully.

Most river fisherman today use either spinning or spincasting reels on rods especially designed for them. The anglers I fish with prefer spinning rods with open-faced reels. The tackle used is rated from light to medium action. I personally use light action rods with reels that are usually considered medium action spooled with a good brand of 10 lb. test line. Most river anglers have special feeling about tackle and line strength.

It is extremely crucial to use two important procedures that spinning tackle gives the angler in fighting fish. The first of these is to use the drag effectively. To understand the drag function on a reel, one must practice pulling line from the rod as a fish would bending the rod as line is pulled from the spool. All spinning reels can be adjusted so that the friction of the gears approaches the breaking point of the line. This adjustment is critical in fighting fish.

The second procedure many experienced anglers use is called back reeling. Most spinning reels have a small switch that can be turned that will permit a reel to be turned backwards as well as forward. The angler can use this backward turning of the reel to enable him to control the fish at the end of the line.

Personally I feel if the friction of the reel's drag is set properly and the angler is patient enough, most fish will be subdued successfully.

The biggest error that anglers commit in fighting fish is to try to overpower fish by using their raw strength. Part of the real pleasure of fishing is to successfully bring to net a fish that is considered too large for the tackle being used.

Most successful rivermen will try to convince their proteges to get good tackle and spend time adjusting the friction of the reel's drag.

Anglers with experience have many memories of large fish lost as a result of making some kind of mistake with their tackle. Poor maintenance, cheap equipment, and careless procedures are all reasons cited for losing the big ones. Twenty-twenty hindsight always provides the right answer.

I believe each of us develops our own fish-fighting methods and will gain confidence as we have more success. It is really interesting to watch others fight fish and consciously consider how you as the angler would handle the same battle.

I would like to conclude this chapter by telling you I learn something new about fighting fish with each trip. Every species of fish has unique fighting characteristic, and you as an angler will learn through experience how best to deal with that. Don't be afraid to learn from your own mistakes.

CHAPTER 18

Getting
Bait

Most bait fishermen consider getting bait as part of the pleasure of fishing. The rivermen I fish with take great pride in providing their own bait and catching fish with that bait. It is similar to the feeling that many hunters get who are successful with their own reloaded ammunition.

The required time, equipment, and expense to collect bait would be possibly considered negative features by many anglers. If an angler feels this way, he should either purchase bait or be a lure fisherman.

Each river system has special features an angler must learn. Anglers preparing to gather bait must be aware of problems that could arise as they net minnows, crayfish, hellgramites, etc.

It is very important fishermen read and know the state regulations concerning live bait. In many cases the numbers of bait fish and fish bait in an angler's possession is limited. Many states regulate the equipment used in catching bait. Anglers should be very careful with these regulations as being ignorant of the laws can be very costly and take away the pleasures of angling.

It is also important to know what hazards might occur in the area you are considering as a place to catch bait. Many dangers can befall an inexperienced person. In Pennsylvania deep water, poisonous snakes, and poison ivy are the most common problems anglers must confront as they net live bait.

The key to using natural bait is getting that bait from tributaries of the river that you plan to fish. It is obvious that the trophy fish in a river system are used to seeing and feeding upon the bait fish found in the watershed.

It is quite easy to see there are a lot of different methods of catching bait throughout the country, and I recommend that a beginning angler or a new angler in a particular river system research how live bait fishermen catch bait in that local area.

CHAPTER 19

Those Rare Times

There are certain instances in many rivers when minnows are not the best choice of bait. The instance foremost in mind is when the river is higher than normal and cloudy or as rivermen say, off color.

It appears most species of gamefish rely on the sense of smell more when the water clarity is bad. Live minnows probably do give off an attractive scent, but several other live bait apparently give off stronger odors.

I have determined when water conditions are as mentioned, river fishermen will be more successful using baits such as hellgramites or crayfish. Several times I tried to continue fishing minnows only to find I caught far less bass than friends fishing the other live baits.

Any angler who has ever fished hellgramites know they really have a strong odor, and in cloudy water this may be an extremely important attractor for fish such as smallmouth bass and channel catfish.

In addition to hellgramites, I believe that crayfish have significant odors that attract fish. If one considers how fish find softshell crayfish even in the darkest night, smell must be the key in this nighttime activity.

During the daylight hours, any river fisherman knows most

crayfish are also more active in cloudy or muddy water, thus being available to fish at these times.

Any fisherman gutting his catch will verify the large consumption of crayfish by almost any species of gamefish. I again emphasize that fish eat so many crayfish because they are plentiful and easily caught.

It is not that the fish have turned off to minnows during extreme water conditions, it is simply that their eyesight is affected and their other senses take over in food foraging. To be successful and to enjoy river fishing, the angler must be able to read the water and determine what natural bait might be more productive and give the fisherman a fun day fishing. A fisherman who cannot adapt will have many frustrating days. Night fishing is another time when bait other than minnows may be good again for the same reasons as mentioned for high cloudy rivers. Some species of fish are also apparently attracted to sounds that duplicate those natural sounds given off by organisms that fish will occasionally feed upon. One must keep in mind that some organisms such as mice or frogs swimming across a pool are readily attracted by game fish probably because of vibrations in the water that the fish recognize. Lures that duplicate these movements will often be good at night. An example of this is the classic jitterbug lure.

As an angler don't be afraid to vary your techniques. Something as simple as changing the number and size of split-shot may make the difference. It is important that an angler know how his quarry's feeding behavior will be affected by the changing water conditions. Always keep in mind that an angler must be willing and able to adjust to changing river conditions whether they are manmade, caused by storms, or simply changing of the seasons.

Note From The Author

It has been my goal to provide the beginning river angler information and general techniques to use and build upon as experiences are gained. In no way do I claim that everything mentioned in this book will work for every angler.

I also hope this book helps individual fisherman gain understanding and appreciation of their river.

If you as an angler have any questions or want to tell me of your river fishing experiences, please feel free to write me at P.O. Box 32, Bellwood, Pennsylvania, 16617.

About The Author

Jerry Sneath is a retired biology teacher. He received both a B.S. and M.Ed. in biology from Pennsylvania State University. As a boy he grew up in Bellwood, Pennsylvania and spent most of his time fishing and hunting along the Juniata River. His love of the outdoors is part of a long family tradition as both his father and grandfather were avid outdoorsmen. Jerry has spent nearly half a century observing nature, teaching others about it and expressing his love for it. Both his experiences and biological training are used in this book.

Jerry's main objective is to get others to value the natural river systems as he does. He believes that as others learn to love and respect wild rivers, only then will they be protected.